The Future Will Call You Something Else

THE

FUTURE

WILL CALL

YOU

SOMETHING

ELSE

NATASHA SAJÉ

Tupelo Press
North Adams, Massachusetts

ISBN 978-1-946482-73-0 (paperback)
ISBN 979-8377415-30-5 (hardcover)

Library of Congress Control Number: 2022936541
Cataloguing-in-Publication data available upon request.

Cover and text designed by Bill Kuch.

First edition September 2023

Tupelo Press
P.O. Box 1767
North Adams, Massachusetts 01247
413-664-9611 / Fax: 413-664-9711
editor@tupelopress.org
www.tupelopress.org

Tupelo Press is an award-winning independent literary press that
publishes fine fiction, non-fiction, and poetry in books that are a joy to
hold as well as read. Tupelo Press is a registered 501(c)(3) non-profit
organization, and we rely on public support to carry out our mission of
publishing extraordinary work that may be outside the realm of the
large commercial publishers. Financial donations are welcome and are
tax deductible.

This project is supported in part by an award
from the National Endowment for the Arts

For Hiltrud Sajé, 1929–2020

reeds bent at the river's mouth
heartsease in snow
aspen as far as

THE FUTURE WILL CALL YOU SOMETHING ELSE

ACKNOWLEDGMENTS

Friends have helped me enormously. I am indebted to the following readers for their insights and feedback: Sara Backer, Catherine Barnett, Robin Becker, Lisa Bickmore, Lauren Camp, Karen Garthe, Kimberly Johnson, Lisa Katz, Madeleine Mysko, Paisley Rekdal, Susan Sample, Jim Schley, Jennifer Tonge. Gratitude to Cyrus Cassells, Amy Gerstler, and David Wojahn for their endorsements, and to the periodical editors who chose these poems for first publication. A special thank you to Patty Paine at Diode Editions for publishing the chapbook *Special Delivery* (2021).

Academy of American Poets Poem-a-Day: The Night Begins with Sugar
America: Against Fireworks
Antioch Review: A Capella
Cavewall: Consideration with Wasp
Copper Nickel: Dear Jolene
Crazyhorse: Brown Velvet Blouse
Epoch: To the Fatherweed
Georgia Review: Palette
Hubbub: The Island
Kenyon Review: A Phrasal Verb Primer
Maine Review: Correspondence
Matter: Journal of Compressed Literature: On Invention
Minnesota Review: Apostrophe
Nonbinary Review: Gradual
On the Seawall: September Swim, The Lure
Painted Bride Quarterly: Is Homosexuality Contagious?, Dear Utah, Dear Caitlyn Jenner
Plume: On Beauty, To the Phaistos Disk
Poetry: Alive
Prairie Schooner: Notes on Elegy, Sonic Icons

Pushcart Prize Anthology 2020: Alive
Rhino: Slipskin
Salamander: The Root of All
Sand and Sky: Poems of Utah: A Meeting
Shearsman Magazine (UK): On Privacy, Ashes of Roses
Shenandoah: To Alfred Hitchcock, in a Dream
Smartish Pace: Repair
Southern Indiana Review: To Alcohol
Sou'wester: Mitti Attar
Spillway: Spiral Jetty
SWWIM: Self Portrait as Tree
Taos Journal of International Poetry and Art: One Difference Between Good and Old
Terrain: To the Twelve Muskrats…
The Arches National Park Reader: A Meeting
Under a Warm Green Linden: One Bud to One Tender Leaf, Palliative
Verse Daily: Dear Jolene, Mitti Attar, To Alcohol

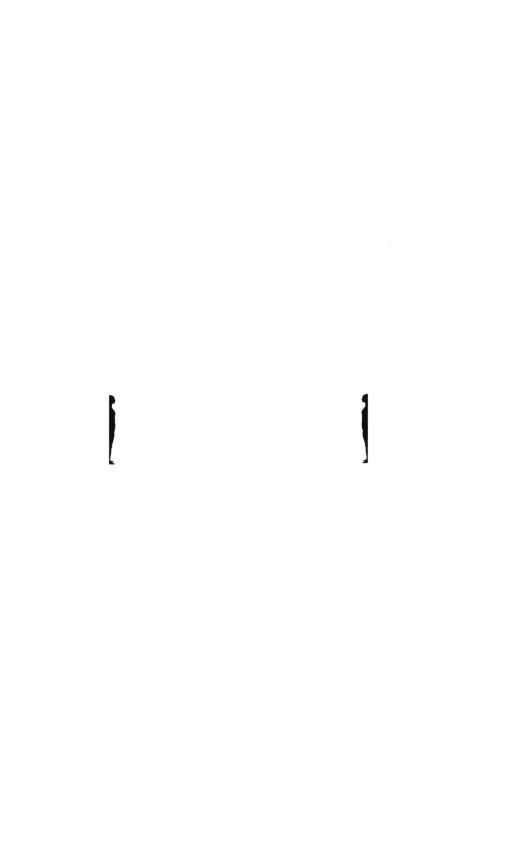

Is Homosexuality Contagious?

Like where you touch a door knob and then wipe your eye and two days later you have a scratchy throat? *Or a restaurant patron*

seeing Baked Alaska at another table flaunt its frosted heat, tender cake under cold fruity creaminess and fluffy mountains of meringue.
You've heard of it.

You're born that way. Either liking women or men or both and in-between. Or neither. Or not knowing or at least not knowing yet. Or wanting to know. Or not.

Watch the person move their spoon into the mound.

The Romans. Look what happened to them.

Mike Pence calls his wife "mother."

Hear a faint smack of lips.

Their daughter wrote a story about a rabbit based on Marlon Brando.

If we're talking about animals, recall the two male penguins who raised an orphan chick. Or the half female-half male cardinal. You could see the split.

That's genetic. Abominations, etc. Can we blame

Augustine who thought he could live without a body and wanted everyone else to do the same.

Yada, yada, yada. Which means "know" in Hebrew. Or to show mercy.

Each of us has things we must turn away from. Look

but don't touch. Think but don't act. Don't think too hard, actually. Feel.

No, don't feel.

The whole room orders the flaming thing.

Because you weren't really hungry.

SLIPSKIN

Baltimore County

On this narrow path along a river
a scent in crisp October air

hangs like a hood. Unmistakable
musk whips my head

toward its source: blotched yellow
wrinkled hairy leaves shield

bloomed dark purple grapes
whose wax rubs off with my thumb.

Someone lived here once, grew fruit in land
razed of forest, allowed sun to sweeten it.

Even in shade the vine still bears
Concord, after Ephraim Bull's northern town

to honor his crossing the vines
Leif Erickson saw on the coast of Vinland:

North American vitis *labrusca* with *vinifera,*
making a fox grape, the odor I ingest

more than three hundred years after natives
were pushed west while Africans

labored for the first Catholic Calverts.
They cleared woods and tilled land,

grew fruit as big as wild plums,
skin that slips off with my teeth,

large seeds I swallow.

To the Fatherweed

bromus tectorum

as I move
one heavy leg then the other
walking in our arid west

everywhere
I see you

furry lavender stems
stirring gracefully in dry air

roots that slip from soil
when grasped
from blanketed fields

leaving countless more

long awns
little blue flames
punishing the mouths of cattle and sheep

in winter you suck snow melt
in summer you burn first
remain flammable longer
come back first after fire

trillions upon trillions of tiny seeds
remain dormant for years

are spread by wind
by animals birds cars water
to desert land

crowding out sagebrush
and without
rabbits have nowhere to hide
and without
eagles have no reason to nest

sage and rabbits and eagles
replaced by swaths of cheatgrass

o pater ignacia
pater venenum
pray for us

your foot soldiers

SPIRAL JETTY

Robert Smithson's earthwork, Great Salt Lake

Not the magnificent coil I imagined
Not worth the discomfort

Of a long bumpy ride on bad roads
Just three curls of black basalt piled

On grey sand and blue lake
Easy to walk on or walk over

An experience I choose not to repeat
Despite a possibly different water level

Variable light or clouds
And ever so slightly eroded rock

I know the jetty will always look
More or less the same
Unlike the first time—what?

The first time I knew my mother
Tired of being in her body
Will soon stop eating

Will stop looking at me with longing
A longing I'll never again not satisfy

TO THE PHAISTOS DISK

1700 B.C.E. Crete, decrypted 2014

If someone then had passed on your words
asking those listeners to tell others, younger,
and the practice had continued,
your spiral of insight

honor and glory to the mother goddess

might have meant more by now.

Instead, you are still not understood.

                In my twenties in the Heraklion
museum I must have seen the symbols
printed on your clay round.
                    Mostly I remember being sick
shivering in April on an attic cot
owned by a woman who gathered tourists at the port.
She drove me and three others past
the cold sea to her small white house

and because I didn't want to share a room
with a strange man—
how would he have read that—

I remember my regret at being female
and fearful of a stranger,
even one interested in antiquities
even one with whom in a different circumstance
I might have had a friendship or an affair.

Wisdom can dissipate like smoke,
but my imprinting, unlike yours,
is understood.

To the Twelve Muskrats Moving in a Line Behind My Chain Link Fence at Dawn in Salt Lake City on the First of September

in the beginning all the world was water

until you   *moskwas*

dove to the depths to gather a ball of mud

blew on it until

it became the whole earth

together this morning for safety

you prepare for the hard freeze

move quietly in the dark of a new moon

you hear glaciers crack thousands of miles away

carry a map of water in the desert

how did you draw it?

how can we read it?

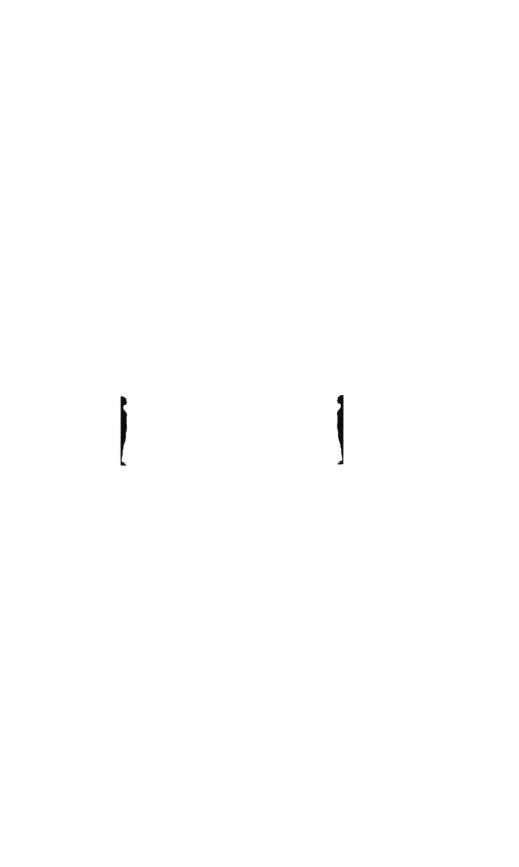

SONIC ICONS

I.

if I say *duvet, night, bed,*
you'll expect you heard *sleep*

if I say *raw, China, worm*
you'll think *silk*

and if I say *I love you, I love you, I love you*
hear *eye olive yew*

II.

hear *olive, tree, silver*
picture four-lobed creamy yellow calyxes

birds later eating all the fruit
hidden by the grey-green leaves

tenacious as hell
bush-tree strangling the fence

a song

III.

sit quietly in the garden in the heat
hear the moon rise
                milk curdle

listen to apples falling from the tree
thud thud   thud

their hearts a little rotten
from worms you never see

IV.

Persian Spring Table

wheat
      rebirth

pudding
        wealth

olive
     love

garlic
      health

apple
      beauty

sumac
       sunrise

vinegar
        long life

V.

a wide and gentle river
that turns so often back upon its course
flanked by fertile land
sweet verbena oleander olive trees
in the soft moist air of evening

our bodies an ancient
waterway not forgotten
concealing its direction
we make grass bend with our voices
east to west to the sea

THE ISLAND

Surely I saw that island once—

Griswold and Watts appear
on a map of the Sound

where two summers I worked
at seventeen and eighteen.

I remember the dream—
stepping onto a gray weathered

dock from a wobbly metal boat—
the green shore sparked with white cottages,

my sneakers on rocks above
killfish and silversides in the shoal

murky with weeds
wrapping my hand like a net.

A distant red cloth flags its pole
in a visit I am not sure happened.

The island is a stone fruit sweetly-
sourly indissoluble from skin,

a realm floating in my mind,
its causeway surrounded

by four hundred miles of vessels
seeking fresh water.

Dear Utah,

State in which I have lived longer
than any other, state of my discontent.
Horace said *skies change,*
souls don't, although like most,
I blame anything but myself.
You are the place where I moved for work
and the place I've complained about
for one-third of my life,
the locus I'm trapped in—
an aging otter in an arid zoo.
You are my theremin—vibrations
and tremors I feel without touch.
Sometimes a fly-over sense
of being left alone, even though
the bank teller calls me by my first name.
We Utahns wear jeans to the symphony
and use family as an excuse
for not showing up. We drive streets wider
than highways while the "blessed"
call the shots, where one in five
carries a gun. I roll my eyes at special
rings and garments that mark
me as having no ward. You are the state
I must explain: watery beer
or restaurants near schools without liquor.
You are also the state where I'm never
lost: your mountains close—gray rock in summer,
whiter in winter, green in May before drought—
tell me where and when I am,
along with the copper mine seen
from space, the salt lake too shallow
to swim, the townhouses jammed into
crevices of valley like aphids on a leaf.
Humans are edged by wilderness

where elk, coyotes, moose, and mountain lions—
and no mosquitos! no mold!—roam.
O Utah, you're a kinky rectangle and I'm a pear
wasted on a December tree.
We're both queer as cupcakes except you
pretend you're white bread.

A Riddle

my mother mimics you
beyond language into sound alone
whooh whooh wheeh

around our inconsistent earth
from which as if punctuating sentences
you rip up trees

farmed and milled but never stopped for good
you're a deity in swirling leaves
worshipped for dynamic draft

a field-befriending fiend
trading in heat and speed
named by directions from which you blow

my mother aches for clarity
in the very way that you
are never misunderstood

alert to the end when our sun will die
you augur toxic or clear
the unseen atmosphere

you force our issue
whatever you bring
we try to forsake

GRADUAL

> "Just one word…plastics."
>> *The Graduate, 1967*

I wrench and cut the clear thick film—
Envisioning its path to trash. And next?
The hiding place where no one ever goes.
This stuff gets smaller and smaller...
Micro to nano to who knows what.
Every way you look at this you lose.
1% of me is probably it
Already, seeding cells with particles,
Through infinitesimal scissor-teeth.
The vision that was planted in my brain.
In Latin, *sapiens* means wise.
The future will call us something else.

Consideration with Wasp

you barely alive   autumn heavy in the western sun
sluggish as a moldy apple
tired of foraging   chewing wood
leaving tramlines in the patio furniture
a papery globe in the eaves

at two I was the source of nectar
wasps built a nest outside my window
dislodged   they swarmed
stung me over and over

fear of flying insects fixed into a scintilla
the need to flee from them
wired into me like a taste for sugar

now you   neither bee nor ant   are the one alone
your compound eyes see me multiply

and you are fading   so exhausted
I could moisten a paper towel and crush you
like a seed pod

your mistake to enter my house
dumb thing

you'll die on your own   unless
you are the queen   large and strong
looking for a place to overwinter

why not my window sash?

CORRESPONDENCE

Dear cottage: my grandparents dwell in you,
bordered by deep beech, spruce, and fir.
Standing on your balcony overflowing
pink and white verbena, they watch me
walk up the gravel path. I've fetched milk,
still warm, from the dairy down the road.
Can you smell the brook where minnows glint
fast over stones toward the shallow Staffelsee,
its peat bog bright with sedge and autumn
crocus? I open the door to your kitchen.
My grandmother has heated water
on the wood stove, poured it into a tin tub
in which I'll bathe.

              Dear 1914 Tudor
Revival with herringbone brick and slate roof:
We feel the heft of forty-seven wooden
windows and doors, the red tile terrace framed
by hemlocks, boxwoods with their oddly
human smell. Built before cars in a suburb
now Baltimore's *inner city*. We restore
you with work that erases other work,
pitch into which we sink. We remove walls,
replace pipes, scrape and paint, sand and wax.
Add daffodils, wild geranium, lavender.
How lovely to sit inside watching rain
drain onto garden plants. Better
still to see it stop. At dusk I stride, keys
sharp in my hand, sirens in the air.
We sell at a loss and move in a hurry,
your promise left behind—

Dear tract house
with a mountain in back: I like your plainness,
your deference to grandeur. We live
quietly. Ermine slink along the stone
wall, coyotes pose on the crest
of the old lake bed. Rocky alkaline
soil. Lemon balm and parsley, myrtle
spurge and cheatgrass. The county sprays
dichlorophenoxyacetic acid
and no one's told. I ask you, is any weed
that bad? Our neighbor's beehives die. I loved
their flowery honey from trumpet vines.
The dead bees—broken paper shells—emit
a scent of musk.

Dear place in which I'll die:
I like to think you will radiate heat
under wood and travertine floors, old woven rugs.
Big windows. On a wall, the painting of two
women just about to kiss. How to live?
I mistyped *love*. A home as hospitable
as wool, though I don't know yet where you'll be.
In the last third of my life I want a dream
real and fixed, a dwelling not obscured
by clouds. And yet I know
I only spend the day—

PALETTE

From a love poem by Montale
I learned about a *bug—cochineal—*

A parasite that eats the red
Fruit of prickly pear

And then becomes the color carmine.
In another book I found

Rose madder: softer
Red, fugitive, from a root

Remnants of which were found in King Tut's tomb.
The teacher who translated Montale also

Loved Indian speeches and Greek plays,
Antonioni's films. He liked us—I won't

Say love, his mixture of respect
And interest. *Bildung* is

Reading with feeling, culture
And history. Education is love

For something beyond the self
Nietzsche said. My love

For color is so intense
I dream of shoes to complement

A dress. Eggplant edged with
Daffodil or pale blue

Striped with hickory. And I recall
My teacher's voice: a cello well

Played with a horsehair bow.
Twenty-five, sipping tea in his living

Room and introduced to—what?
I had no garden then. But studied:

Pallet from straw, palate
For the roof of the mouth.

I know the difference between
These words—and so? Someday

I'll forget the color Vermeer used
For Mary's blouse or why it matters.

My teacher died at the age I am now
Thirty years ago. I wish I could tell him

I've eaten prickly pear and seen
Cochineal. And that he made

Me feel a pull like gravity
But from the sky.

Dear R

When the grad student called your work "spry"
in the introduction, at the podium
you ignored *nimble, energetic,* and *brisk,* and
lamented, "spry is for old people,"
detouring into slack skin and liver spots.
At forty-nine, you look young to me;
I'm sixty-five. You make fiction,
I make poems, gathered into books few
people buy. Later I read interviews, curious
if under your smooth face might be worry
over being *glib,* a less flattering
Germanic monosyllable. I also fret,
anxious I'm out of time to *fail better.*
Mediocrity means toiling over words
like a jailor whose prisoners are dead,
but perhaps our grave self-doubts
save us from even more mistakes. Recall
Nahum Tate's rewrite of *Lear* reigning
for a hundred years, or presidents whose confidence
covers vacuity. Dear R, acclaim is
a psychological chew toy, and if
our jaws are empty, we might gnaw instead
on our irrelevance, fed by the fact that
along with one-quarter of the earth's population,
we have a gift for words, albeit
not always the discernment of when
and how to use them.

PALLIATIVE

pallium
the cloak that covers the body on its way to burial

a cloth of comfort

comfort once meant strong and now
means soft and easeful

as in morphine and mouth sponges
as in care
as in acquiring at the end

the cloak
clocca   bell-shaped

as when the world was quieter
and the sound of a bell
could ring in an afterlife

I'd like to begin anticipating
my body as a sponge
filled and wrung out again and again
by pain and the will to live

palliative
                        not *pale*

as in beyond the
staked vines on a fence dividing
governable from wild

known from unknown

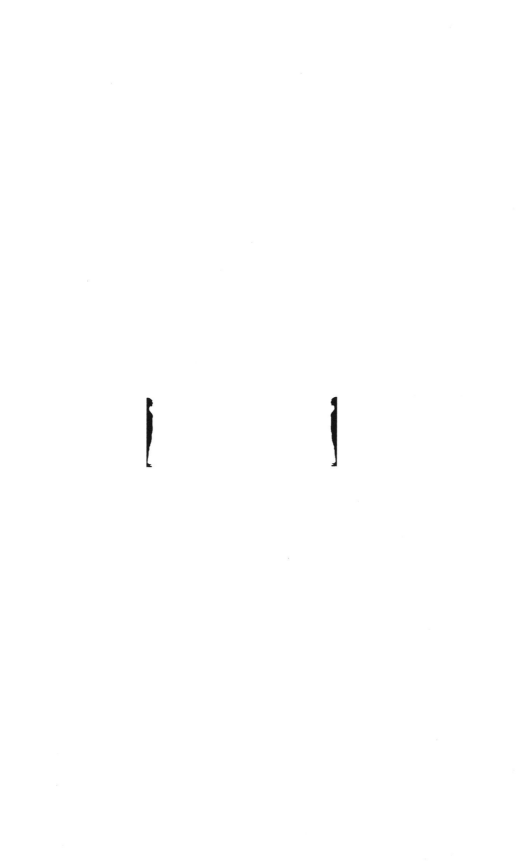

A Phrasal Verb Primer

you and I did not use up   (what we had)
I looked after   (you) (myself)
you went through   (who can know)
after you ran out   (of time)
I turned down   (sheets) (nothing)
I am getting on with   (a new life) (a wife)
you made sure of   (the setting sun in a crimson sky)   (a watermark moon)
what can add up to   (a memory) (forgetting)
I give back   (what you gave me) (to someone else)
I do over   (better) (with more or less heart)
let me spell out   (guilt)
don't look over   (here) (at us)
I'll go on   (as long as I live)
and answer to   (no one) (myself)

THE NIGHT BEGINS WITH SUGAR

Salt Lake City

in a theocracy of pretense and defense
a state of smog   of smug

crystalline over mountains and horizon melt
such pretty clouds   such drifting light

who is it enough for   what kind of person

lives in this sweetness   this clear
beauty and does not utter a single oh

catching malaise
a coma of indifference

swirling in our stunning vestibule
mourning the self just getting by

Reading

I'm bundled in another mind
as if it were a down coat

the world thick and quiet

neurons coax
words like insects

grant them legs and wings

a swarm that rouses me

on the train or the plane
in the meadow on the beach or in bed

words riddle a raft
full of tiny holes

so I can float

Self-Portrait as Tree

Sometimes I am evergreen, generous as a bosom, blossoms creamy as a satin blouse spread glossy and fragrant on a mansion's thick lawn. The green leaves shine metallic, but alive, alive. I'm the queen of gratification, the princess of the instant. On those days my knees don't hurt, I could build a house. Other days, my leaves are doomed to fall. I'm the pawn of a waning half-moon, time and promise dwindling. My roots protrude, dry and close to the surface, gnarly dark. My life swings on a hammock as I sleep and read, read and sleep, making paper out of hardwood, consuming myself at the same time that I inscribe myself.

Dear Caitlyn Jenner,

You say, *there's more to being*
a woman than hair and makeup.
What: swaying walk, tender heart?
My wife likes polish now and then—
a woman who's never worn pink
or a push up bra. In the pool,
scarlet toes make me look twice,
the color glints like blood. I look
and look again, as when I eye your shift
from Bruce to Cait—your lifelong dream lived late—

I will be able to live authentically
as female, but I've missed so much.
Authentic: from one's own authority.
It's quite a dream to have a body that
does not get in the way of who we are.
I cleaned the whole closet out—the boys' stuff
is gone. You wear your heart, let arrows
pierce it. My method is blending in.
No gazing in the glass, and as I age,
I'm ever more invisible. Still,

it's a different thing to take down
womanhood instead of build it
from scratch, a line drawn in the dirt.
I'd like to start anew. I'm a crumbling
bridge between who I am and what I like.
I wouldn't mind losing the breasts,
their squish, their sag and flop—
but what would balance skillet-wide hips
and buttocks round as cabbages?
I'd shrink those too. I'd choose a boy's
narrow pelvis, flat chest, muscled.

Yours, before, come to think of it.
Note we both said "boy," youth and power
in every move. I don't have to justify.
When every body is a field of claim,
differences aren't small. I know the itch
to float, to choose my sex and who I love
as I choose clothes, each day a palette
or a lump of clay. You want *to be yourself,*
get dressed, get ready to go out, and just
be like a normal person. I take for granted
what you've never had. Fairness
depends on where we start.

THE ROOT OF ALL

burns a hole in your head
sprouts wings and flies
won't bark up the right

unless you shell out or marry it
hand over fist penny wise or not
occasionally pound dumb

after a certain yearly sum it can't buy
you know what but up to then
finders keepers losers

reapers picking millet from a field
or apples from the cart upset
during short sell and hell to pay

someday not today I'll take
bruised ones fallen
into gutters so as not to lose

my skirt or need to pluck
a tin spoon from a sow's ear
I want more but won't bite

the fingers that squeeze me
time is not blood from a turnip
so pay as you go or go as you wish

chew the bacon
and bring it home like my hand-
knit sweater bought on thrift

that will burn when I do
since it can't pass
through the eye of a needle

BROWN VELVET BLOUSE

candlelight and a deeper honey
backs of hibernating bees
my extravagant small yet bearish pleasure
late winter's glint and shimmer
climbs a stair   holds a walnut rail
and in the mirror of the season admires its
flourishing warmth

I am a sheared cat   sleepy
whose front legs exactly fit her paws
buttons light as chips of tooth
tightly sewn to queenly cloth
the holes just so   they take a wily finger

now I must undress *now*
not another minute in this pelt
instead of unbuttoning   pull over my head

                                        it rips

and marks spring's molt and fluster

ASHES OF ROSES

I.

no one wears it today   this Victorian shade
with more than a hint of mourning
more than a hint of love
petals and rock face clad in moon
white heat in cinders of extinguished fires
a precious stone occluded
morganite perhaps
nuance of odd blend and whir
this cousin of regret   this mute and lighter form of ill
corolla of sweetness with an edible petiole

II.

of all which passed the feeling only stays
of a cap knitted for me by my godmother
in angora   the soft pink rim and lamb's wool   the gray rest
a thing of animal for animal
my baby head captived
so that a lifetime later I recall it
not at all in shadow

ON BEAUTY

*

I have a tree outside my house. I don't know what kind—in spring, it blooms, gorgeous. Pink flowers clustered together, as big as a small dog.

*

Anne Frank looked upon the horse chestnut outside her window and wrote, *on whose branches little raindrops shine appearing like silver.* That was winter and she could make something out of nothing.

*

In the summer there's fruit on my tree, green globes with short spikes like a medieval weapon. They fall to the ground and break open. Inside: shiny red nuts—hard and unblemished. I could string them.

*

My tree's a horse chestnut. If only I had the true kind, edible. I'd water that tree in a drought. I'd pick the nuts as soon as they fell. I wouldn't want the weevils to get them first. I'd score and roast them, simmer them in sugar syrup to make them swell and last.

*

An old chestnut. I don't mind hearing a certain story again and again.

*

The monkey promises the cat a share of chestnuts if she'll pull them from the fire. She does, and burns her paws, and the wicked clever monkey eats them all: *Tirer les marrons du feu.*

*

Aesculus hippocastanum, because the fruit was thought to cure horses of lung ailments. If only I had a horse. I could cut this tree down, but the wood's too soft. What's it good for?

*

Under my feet and tires, the sound of crumbling yellow leaves.
Shall I take a picture for you?

SEPTEMBER SWIM

Heidegger's fourfold: earth, sky, mortals, divinity

in thrall to sun & heat the last sweet
slavish love of summer
body skimming half immersed

recalls forty years before
another pool
another country

a curved hillside & houses
whose function is style

spared bombing
but not neglect

peeling paint & rusted metal
impressed on me *dwelling*
as in the need *to be*

alone I admired architecture
wishing anyone would open a door
invite me in   no one did

I went swimming
not knowing the engine
inside my ribs

what it could lose
what it might attain

A MEETING

Arches National Park

here
      where the river flooded and wore
through Jurassic rock a channel

we reconsider   empty
from Old English

the"p"a euphonic insertion
language and leisure filled

to help us make sense of our senses
as now in red sand with a dusting of snow

I see the print of my boots
hear the thrum of salt thousands of feet thick

smell sunlight like carbonation in the air

replete with sharp stars

AGAINST FIREWORKS

we huddle for the blazing
man-made strident colored stars
shot with cannons
propelled by rockets

they last seconds
then dissipate like apologies

we sign off on the noise
on costs and damages

wouldn't we do better to love
a face   any face   a dog's

Notes on Elegy

I.

what would I have been without you?
maybe less   perhaps more

a wasp's nest under a porch corner
papery   layered   combed
geometric   and fragile

I'll never know
if you kept me from stinging
or swelling

II.

days since I looked in a mirror
probably best
not to see the ravage of burst capillaries
eyes shattered red

once grief   now
illness   same result

I bathe my eyes in darkness

in sleep also I see sanguine
organs   a web of vessels
crossed and woven

a banyan tree
seeming to exist on nothing but air

roots grow up and down
as well as sideways

with hovering
humming and crawling creatures

packed as if into a small city zoo
but free to wander

ONE BUD TO ONE TENDER LEAF

after Lu Tong

on lion peak mountain
evergreen forests are fed by dreaming-of-the-tiger-spring
in soft mist
                                a wind

weng shang yi is eighty-four
fingers blistered from frying tea
his face a round saucer
                                a wind hurries

his wife picks the leaves
by the fifteenth day before spring equinox
tomb sweeping day
                                a wind hurries my wings

for an hour the fresh leaves wither
then are fried then rest then are fried then rest and after
the third and final fire   barely damp

                                a wind hurries my wings toward

no thirst   no sadness   all is fair
each body's language of sinew and bone
touching other worlds
                                a wind hurries my wings toward heaven

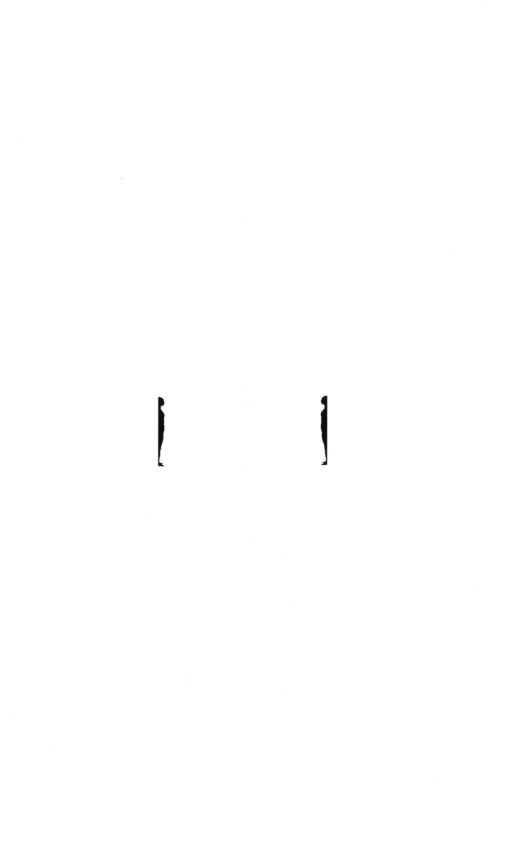

APOSTROPHE

I.

I'm a tad sorry for you   floating mark
often forgotten or in the wrong place
trivial as lint

a currant in a muffin
sweet in the way that being correct is sweet

II.

for years I circled *its'* on student papers
explaining that *its'*
like *irregardless* does not exist

now I often let error stand

marks only sometimes useful
in this economy we've made

III.

in English the apostrophe developed a voluminous appetite
for possession not just elision

swallowing *es*

womman is mannes joye and al his blis

IV.

savvy printers saving time and type
changed the way we scribe and snipe
til we be roten, kan we nat be rype

V.

you might understand
when I rue myself

and turn
neck tucked into torso
limb at a right angle

a flamingo sleeping on one leg
still a body

a gust of wind could topple

One Difference Between Good and Old

I thought of distant friends
like hotels, open for me
to check in with my new clothes
and same smile. I thought
next year will be time enough,
plenty of time, that cornucopia.
Our shared history—we stole fruit,
broke into the daycare,
vexed the boss, slid down
the mountain in an inner tube—
would wait, I thought,
like the ocean between us.

I should have known, thinking
about the apples I like to eat
for breakfast, one season after another,
that a letter is not a visit. And now
there's no next winter or summer, no
goodbye. Now gone to me—*me,*
me, this is not an elegy although
I've lost a person in whom
was lodged a stripe of myself.
A suit altered entirely from what
I was counting on in my foolishness.

Dear Fate

I'll choose the spice from the row
above the sink—Grains of Paradise or
Malabar pepper, black, to season this
equinox eight weeks before winter. You'll
decide when I die, when my body
dissolves into lye. Your wind
topples indigenous oaks, not only
pines planted in shallow soil. For now,
you allow me to live, like a fizzing
molecule in a glass of Prosecco.
Hail, happiness. Hello house of deafness
where I listen for what comes next while
calculating the hours I spend
in anticipation. The best and worst
thing about you, Fate, is that you don't
fall into a pattern like a nineteenth-
century novel or for that matter,
my own self-image. Your affection
flickers, a loose eyelash. Your
indifference is divine.

SILENCE

in my house so quietly set
between mountains and what I think of as an obedient city
I've become insulated

from drivers blowing their horns
instead of going to the front door

from construction trucks and cranes
     helicopters   sirens
all day and all night long

not to mention car parts wrappers hair dead animals
chicken bones crumbled curbs and brick orange DoT cones
clothing lead pipes bent street signs

noise behind my eyes

along with people with mental or substance problems
who roam aimlessly panhandle steal
urinate rifle through garbage hide in bushes
sleep in alleys yell when I pass

I would rather not smell or see
or hear them

no angry no pleading voices
no gunshots no screams no blood

     you don't want it to happen
     or you don't want to hear it or see it?

both?
if it doesn't happen I won't hear it

it's been so long since I was exposed

yet I am sick of suburbs
                                    of surface docility

                    autoimmune spirit

if someone is at my door it's at my request
whatever I say
from behind the peephole my whole
truth
                                    and nothing but

as I slide into old age I retreat

explain and excuse
the isolation I cherish

when instead it might be my privilege to

quicken on streets
rub shoulders with people I don't know

hold up a placard and yell
with a crowd where I'm one of many who believe
it's risky to stand

conditions must change or else

                    that's not silence

no

Dear Roe v. Wade,

What a mess you're in, with red states
eroding you like sand under a power
wash of illogical laws, turning back time
to Texas, 1969. I feel for women
in Mississippi, listening to a doctor lie
that abortions cause breast cancer,

and that the fetus can feel pain,
women waiting at the only clinic in the state.
Dangerous, this "personhood," this lie
extending to an embryo the powers
not accorded to the breathing women
who care for and carry it over months.

In 1973, I turned 18.
I appreciate your gloss on "do no harm,"
on history: in 1787 women
were in this way less constrained by states
than corpses are today; they can be forced
to give birth. For whom is that the truth?

We've made the Constitution our true
guide, plus amendments carved in time:
liberty and privacy inherent rights
for every citizen, even those as poor
as Norma McCorvey (Roe), whose statement
on the case reversed, pro to con, for women.

Yet privacy's a cloud with women's
lives hovering like drops of rain. The truth:
so many tears. Thanks to DNA, the state
knows everywhere we go, and sometimes, when.
If you had feelings, Roe v. Wade, you'd be blue,
but you're a court case, judicial law,

one that even Sarah Palin knows.
Irrelevance is cruel, and thinking women
feel their bodies occupied by menace
while living in our land of lies.
I availed myself of you at 29
and for access, I thank Maryland, my state.

Personhood depends on power, and truth
changes like a woman's chance to thrive
within her gendered state, her malady.

ON PRIVACY

our neighbor again drives drunk
this time not
over the flowers in our yard

this time on the highway   crash
landing in the ICU

toes lost to gangrene   a gangly loping walk
and what part of his mind to
nothing to do nothing to do but drink

and then get into his big orange truck

his wife closes the conversation
I feel I am thrusting myself into

a thick hedge

breathing its broken woody scent
peering through crinkled leaves

to the empty pint bottle of Popov glinting from the curb

privacy once meant the *lack of public significance*
to not count or be counted

now in moist November soil
the penstemon seeds itself
around shards of glass

To Alcohol

I.

I remember the stale smell of urine and skin
in the heat of the boiler room

my superintendent father's broom
shooing out two men

bums he called them to my mother
who scrubbed the floor with bleach

and years later a party where my father
drank so much he
couldn't fit the key into the car door

my mother begging *let me drive*
me in the backseat not knowing

alcohol had reduced the force
at which his heart beat
and was seeping into his lungs
to fill our vehicle with haze

II.

in excess everything is poison
even kale or water
I could live without vodka brandy

rum without vanilla extract without beer
and more sadly without wine
and its inspiring

you've never hung me over
although one night in a hilltop restaurant
after a waiter plied me with five courses

and five glasses of wine
I refused to pay a bet I lost

waving my arms like fumes
I did not like the person I became

you are ready and waiting
any time of the year or day

if only science would make yeast not
ferment sugar surely easier
than cloning sheep or curing Ebola

leavened bread a small sacrifice
for reimagining the earth

as ancient north America or Australia
where tribes had no brewing

you are a clump of soft fur
at the back of the throat
music that shifts from ditty to dirge

I suspect my gripe is not with you
but with the fact that humans
are not only the animals

who often don't know when to stop
but are also the only
animals who understand why they can't

Repair

The front arms of the navy blue couch, where the cat loosened acrylic weave into an ugly snaggle of thread. The cat determined to mark her place—her shoulders strong. My stitches shine in brighter blue.

November geranium in the house, dry, pungent, and crumpled brown. I loved its coral flowers, reminders of a sea. With careful pruning and some water, the roots might last until spring.

Why didn't you come? I was too sad. *I needed you. Your sadness should be the reason you'd understand mine.* I'm as solitary as the moon. Clouded as my mother's eyes by cataracts.

Another meaning: "to go," Late Latin, *repatriare,* "return to one's own country." Could mending be gold to glue the crack? I give my gold and ask who might do the work.

It's me, I know, along with you.

To the City of the Future

in crisp morning light in soft afternoon in deep
violet evening you say
I will be here

in granite   marble   and steel

you could be humanity's greatest creation
as Libeskind believes

the best of all possible
or only for the rich

your wide boulevards and avenues
secret ulicas and rues   orderly Strassen
alleys and arcades

the odeon the forum the agora the plaza
where we bump shoulder to shoulder ankle to ankle

without cushions in trains
their screeching brakes and clanging horns

you are patched of places I've been
pieces I can't make whole

five year old dancer with castanets

cellist around a blind corner

bakery's smell of braided butter and spice

sculpture from a car door and a flag pole

Safdie says after the automobile
most of us will live within your limits

gone the little dairy farm
hard to find the forest lane
quietude a fever dream

we'll mix into your crash and clash

all the while
sunning itself on concrete
surrounded by weeds
a brazen scrappy goat
clinks its bell   shakes its head   disturbs flies

ruminates and chews

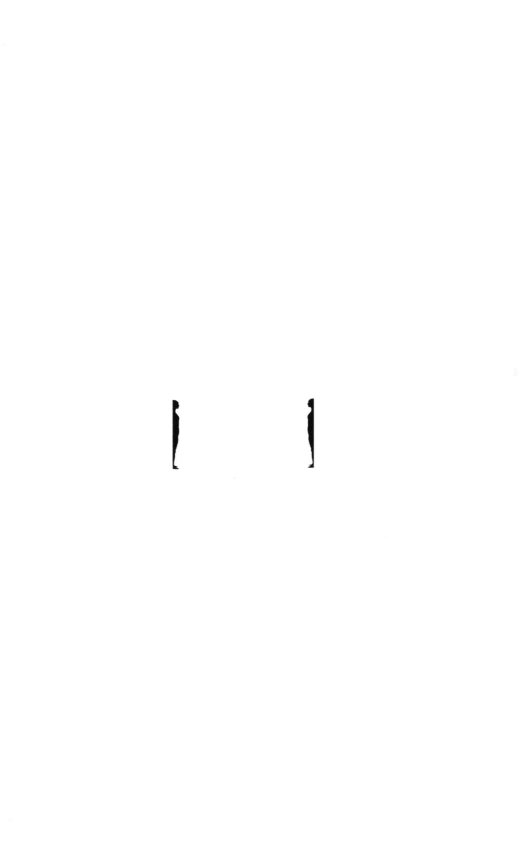

Real Things

I'm food shopping
hands eyes and payment ready

not to mention a loaf the end of which
I'm already chewing off in the grocery

a word with echoes

gross in German means large
in English the value of goods and services

or a dozen dozen or
see what I'm fingering

things knot themselves in lingo
I untie

we say about a car *turn on a dime*
our smallest coin the ground for a vehicle

day is my favorite light
high noon   no shadow

bright like lemon on grilled squash

not quite English is my favored tongue
pilfering off kilter

born that way or made
I'm happy to be fringe

I trim my eyebrows
first brushing the hairs upward
the way at dusk a rat runs up a coconut tree

I'll show you how big with my palms

The Lure

I feel your sadness pour like tar
the darkness worries me

reminiscent of my mother
manipulation *ur*
you do it all forlorn

please you say *a cure*
as if I could close your wound

with fine silk thread   couture
a needle so minute the pricks
are pleasure not unlike champagne

such sewing could take years
and in that time you'll moor
me in a deeper pit

for sure   it's flattering
to leave a spoor

a sticky grandiose allure
flammable and pure

but worth the torment
I'll endure?

Mitti Attar

the scent of first rain on stone
geosmin or petrichor

can be taken from ground near
a lake in Kannauj India after a monsoon

can be bottled and sold
dabbed behind one's ears

we're wired to detect it
in minuscule quantities

this odor we once needed
to find food in times of drought

today we drive to the market
buy Chilean apples in June

lamb from Australia
we order

and soon Mongolian cashmere
is delivered in a plastic envelope by truck

still the smell of rain on dry earth
asks me if I could be every drop

that hits black earth or red rock
even construction debris

the smell asks me
not what I want

but what I am

A Capella

Luther opposed instruments
Zwingli burned organs
in the chapel only the human voice only one voice
to magnify and linger

in the chapel
as in St. Martin's miraculous purity

in the manner of the chapel
resounding overtones
coming from God knows where
the building itself   the cosmos

no lutes or lyres in the chapel
no organ but the throat
imbued with spirit   subdued by mind

windpipe we say
for the body part through which tones pass
bellowed lungs below

no wood or metal here
austere
hardly any wind or water

no fanfare no instrument no melding
no chant no chat no clap

a chill
as sound waves shrink into space

ON INVENTION

italics from *The Most Excellent Book of Cookery (France, 1555)*
trans. Timothy Tomasik and Ken Albala

Counterfeit Snow: First a quart of good rich milk. Make sure it has been a year since the cow had a calf. Add six egg whites, one ounce of rice flour, a quarter pound of powdered sugar, whip together like butter. Skim off what comes to the top. That's the snow. Put it on a plate.

Travel the little tunnel that spans from known to un. Run out of air and breathe anyway.

Peacock and Capon Barded Like Porcupines: Find the slenderest cinnamon sticks, cover in sugar like candy, as long as three or four fingers. Pierce them into said game like the spines of a porcupine. Place the sauce at the bottom of the bowl, making sure it does not touch.

Put a finger in the fish tank and an angel brushes by. Or a sharklet.

Milk jasper: Nice rich milk and the same amount of egg whites. Add chopped parsley, white powder, salt. Mix and simmer and when you have stirred it well, squeeze it in a cloth after it has cooked for a day. Then cut it into slices and fry in butter.

Which flowers are edible? You could be frugal and grow your own. Or forage. Constraints are as useful as bones.

A bowl of elderflowers and as many red roses. Put them into boil and then strain them. Add to this some fine flour, eight egg yolks, two or three ounces of sugar, and a quarter ounce of cinnamon. A bit of powdered saffron, a bit of salt. Mix together and fry as you would other fritters.

The Puritans named girls Patience and Tace, which means be silent. Use your tongue for tasting, your hands for cooking and writing. Both for love.

Take marrow, take rhubarb, take plantain, shepherd's purse and a little comfrey.
Anoint your hands with this and then you can place them into boiling water.

Make a rule.

There should not be cloves with shad nor with fried eggs.

Then break it.

To Alfred Hitchcock, in a Dream

You're speaking in my auditorium
while showing clips—black and white—
your English accent almost drowning
the words, like rocks muddled in water.
A bit perturbed but your points sharp and I'm
listening, rapt, then with a quick shock realize
that it was my job to get you from the airport.
It's four p.m. and I also forgot to provide
breakfast or lunch and you're on stage, bravely
discussing foreboding and foreshadowing.
Suspense is not horror, surprise, or fear.
It's the long agony of figuring out
the real threat. Of waiting for
the inevitable. There you are, a very old
person who managed to get to a strange place
at my request and without my help.
When the talk ends, I walk up to you
to apologize at the same time that I covet
your black alpaca jacket. *I need a drink,*
you say, wiping your brow, and I think I don't
want a drink and I also don't want to take
you to dinner since I just ate lunch. What
I want is for you to disappear like a victim
but you're mine. My arms feel coated in cast iron.
At that moment I wake to a flood of sun,
my heart beating blood warm through my limbs,
and after a moment of mulling,
I think of my senile mother and the drink
she might need and can't ask for.
And then I'm sitting up in bed
as if on a playground bench, with my back
to a jungle gym covered with crows.

Dear Jolene,

You don't know me, or rather you know me
only as one of the women who jog
in the pool you manage, a pool with mostly old people
and children, in 87 degree water that keeps
away serious swimmers. But I have come to know you
albeit in a relentlessly odd way
because while I'm there with my head out of water
and my glasses on, I like to look around
and for four years I've heard and watched you—your
great haircut and dye job—the brown under the blonde
in your case and my opinion quite chic. The bob suits
your square jaw. You like to blow the whistle
on miscreants talking in lap lanes
or running on the deck. This embarrassed another
water jogger so much she stopped coming.
When you did it to me, it piqued
my interest. I too like to keep people
in line. When I see someone using a handicapped
parking spot and walking very well indeed, I say
something! This could get me into trouble, I know,
but I've got gray hair so maybe not.
This letter is a different kind of trouble.
"Trouble," turbid,
cloudy, appropriate for a body of water in which
nearly every swimmer pees. The whole
world is murky sometimes, most of all the people in it.
What do I know? How sweet you are giving a lesson
to a three-year-old and her mother—you clearly
like your job imparting the joy of floatation.
And you've kept fit, albeit
a weight gain of fifteen or so pounds,
distributed evenly. You cover up more quickly
now, so I expect you're self-conscious. I used to be,
before I channeled my 92-year-old aunt, minus

two breasts and wrinkled all the way to the bone.
Menopause requires a shift in eating
habits. I skip dinner a few times a week.
You take out from Jasmine on Thursday nights,
sprinting into your glass-walled office
with white and red plastic bags in your hands,
then closing the blinds. Paying attention is a kind of love,
Jolene, although I'm not attracted to you,
not after that first year when the Internet told me
you moved to Utah for college, married Jared,
bought a three bedroom house and had two children,
a daughter who should be 21 now, although I can't find her
online. A son born two years later.
Twelve years ago you were quoted in a newspaper
about the difficulty of keeping children safe.
More recently, a sister-in-law died mysteriously
in a canyon, her remains found years later.
I wonder about Jared, installing floors all day
and then sitting in the high school gym bleachers,
cheering your son. You loved your grandpa's
silver dollar pancakes and still use the steamer
he gave you in Elmira, but I wonder whether
you're happy, whether your life turned out
the way you dreamed, what you dreamed.
You're a registered Republican, Jolene,
not surprising in light of Jared's Mormonism,
although your Catholicism gave you, we could say,
more choice. I expect we're on opposite
sides of most issues, including whether water joggers
should be allowed to use lap lanes. I give to Planned Parenthood,
your donations are a mystery. I wonder why I care—
should I get a waterproof ipod and listen to *Serial?*
Is my biographical impulse merely learning
facts and constructing a narrative?
A version of reading, like prognostication, intuiting the divine?
Whatever my purpose, I assure you it is not evil.
Freud might ascribe it to loneliness,

an only childhood. Jung might call you a shadow.
Or this could be *my letter to the world that never wrote to me.*
I've written letters to others who won't write
back—the Phaistos disk, Caitlyn Jenner, alcohol—
spilling secrets in poems—works of imagination,
mind you, not journalism—fearing all the while
that the worst thing in life might be
to not be known at all.

ALIVE

You and me, of course, and the animals
we feed and then slaughter. The boxelder
bug with its dot of red, yeast in the air
making bread and wine, bacteria
in yoghurt, carrots, the apple tree,
each white blossom. And rock, which lives
so slowly it's hard to imagine it
as sand then glass. A sea called dead is one that
will not mirror us. We think as human
beings we deserve every last thing. Say
the element copper. Incandescence
glowing bright and soft like Venus.
Ductile as a shewolf's eyes pigmented red
or green, exposed to acid in the air.
Copper primes your liver, its mines leach lead
and arsenic. Smelting is to melting
the way smite is to mite. A violence
of extraction. What's lost when a language
dies? When its tropes oppose our own?
In the at-risk Aymara
the past stretches out in front, the future
lags behind. Imagine being led
by knowing, imagine the end as clear.